SAILIN

The Beginner's Guide to Sailing and Planning your First Sailing Adventure

Kurt Fenton

SAILING

The Beginner's Guide to Sailing and Planning your First Sailing Adventure

Introduction

I want to thank you and congratulate you for downloading the book, *"A Beginners Guide to Sailing"*.

This book contains proven steps and strategies on how to plan for your first sailing adventure.

Sailing is an international sport that offers many rewards. Imagine white sails billowing against a clear sky, the brisk feel of the breeze on your face, and the gentle motions of the boat as it cleanly slices through the water.

While sailing is a great way to enjoy the outdoors, it also requires you to be an active participant more than almost any other type of boating. When you learn how to sail, you'll not only become intimately familiar with all aspects of your boat, but also how your boat relates to its environment in terms of everything from the wind to the weather.

Sailing can be terrific exercise that is both invigorating and relaxing.

Thanks again for downloading this book, I hope you enjoy it!

Chapter 1:

Sailing Terminology

As a beginner to sailing, it can be both exciting and overwhelming to step into the world of sailing. Your first sailing adventure will require a lot of preparation, which I hope to explain in this book. Knowing the basic concepts behind sailing and some basic terminology will go a long way in making your first sailing adventure a successful one.

The world of sailing has its own lingo. Some sailing terms have crossed over and become terms commonly used in everyday discussions. It is vital you know this lingo so you can communicate effectively and safely while sailing with others. Knowing these terms will aid in a successful voyage.

A few basic terms will go a long way when you begin your first sailing adventure. Common sailing terminology is often directional. Sailors use these terms to communicate boat, water, and, spatial conditions to each other.

First, let's start with term "**Bow**". Bow is the term used to talk about and describe the front of the boat. On the opposite side we have the term "**Aft**". Aft is used to describe the back of the boat. Another term that you might more commonly hear to describe the back of a boat on your first sailing adventure is the term "**Stern**". Aft and stern are interchangeable terms to describe the back of the boat.

Another sailing term important for your first sailing adventure is the term "**Port**". Port is the left-hand side of the boat when you are facing the bow. Now, when you are actually on a boat "left" and "right" can become confusing depending on the direction you are facing. Add to this sailing in open waters and one can easy become confused directionally. The term port is always used to define the left-hand side of the boat as it relates to the bow, or front of the boat.

The opposite of Port is the term "**Starboard**". Starboard is the right side of the boat. Again, because one can easily become directionally confused when on a boat at sea, the right side or starboard side of the boat is always oriented in relationship to the front of the boat.

When sailing, weather conditions are a huge factor especially the direction and strength of the wind. A very common and important sail term to know is the word "**Windward**". This term refers to the direction in which the wind is currently blowing. Sailboats tend to move with the wind, making the windward direction an important sailing term to know. The opposite of windward is the word "leeward". Leeward is simply the opposite direction from which the wind is currently blowing.

The term "**Tacking**" is another important basic sailing term you will want to know. Tacking is the term used to describe a basic sailing maneuver. Tacking refers to turning the bow, or front of the boat through the wind so that the wind changes from one side of the boat to the other side. It is the action of turning the bow of a sailboat through the wind so the sail will fill on the other side of the boat.

The opposite of tacking is "**Jibing**". Jibing is a basic sailing maneuver. The term refers to turning the stern or back of the boat through the wind so that the wind changes from one side of the boat to the other side. The boom of a boat will always shift from one side to the other when performing a tack or a jibe. Though both techniques are used to turn a boat or ship, jibing is a less common sailing technique. Since it involves turning a boat directly into the wind it can be a harder technique to successfully accomplish the desired change in course.

In addition to know basic terms regarding wind direction and spatial directions, it is very important to know some basic sailing terms that refer to parts of a sailboat.

One of the most basic terms you will hear on a sailboat is the term mast. The 'Mast' is a tall pole running upright in direction. Usually the mast is referring to the pole centrally located on the deck of a ship. The mast is used to carry and support sails.

Off of the mast you will find the "Boom". The boom is a log pole that is attached to the bottom of the mast horizontally. The boom branches off of the mast and the sail is attached to both the boom and the mast. The boom's location is adjusted to adjust the sails. This is one of the primary ways in which a sailboat uses the wind to control movement. The boom is adjusted towards the direction of the wind so that the sailboat is able to harness wind power in order to move forward or backwards.

Another very important sailing term that will be used during your first sailing adventure is the term "Rudder". The rudder is located beneath the boat. The rudder is a flat piece of wood, fiberglass, or metal that is vertical to the bottom of the boat. The rudder is controlled via a helm and is used to steer the ship. Larger sailboats control the rudder via a helm or wheel, while smaller sailboats will have a steering mechanism directly behind the boat. These are usually switches or handles which directly maneuver the rudder.

Keel is built into the base of the boat. Often the keel projects from the bottom of the boat. It runs the length of the ship or boat and has several purposes. Because it projects from the bottom of the boat, it prevents the boat from being blown sideways by the wind by providing resistance. Also, the keel holds the ballast and keeps the boat upright. This is where the sailboats '**Weight**' is in order to provide stability and draft to the boat.

Chapter 2:

Sailing Concepts

Now that you know a few basic directional terms and parts of a sailboat, it is important to understand the concept of sailing. Sailboats use sails to capture the wind and harness its energy. This energy is used to move the sailboat across water. Sailing involves constantly adjusting the parts of a sailboat and its directional location in order to gain the most momentum from the wind.

When properly trimmed or adjusted, the sail's leading edge is the one which points into the wind. This positioning creates higher pressure on the windward side (the side facing the wind) and lower pressure on the leeward side (the side away from the wind)."

The sail "lifts," or moves, toward the lower-pressure side causing the boat to move. This movement is actually created because the sail isn't a flat sheet of cloth. Sails are purposely designed to be curved to create a draft. The lift is created by the wind blowing across the sails. Not all of the lift developed by a sail moves the boat ahead. Some of the lift tries to pull the boat sideways too. This is where some of the vital parts of a ship come in to play. The hull, keel, and rudder all work together to create resistance to the sideways force. This resistance actually drives the boat forward instead. Due to this design and interaction, sailboats often move both forward and sideways simultaneously.

When steering a sailboat, the more the sailboat steers toward the wind direction, the more you will need to trim or adjust the sails. The sails should be adjusted in tighter to keep them full, and keep generating lift. If sails are adjusted too close to the wind the opposite will actually take place. The sail will "luff"— the forward edge will start to flutter in and out and the boat will slow down. Turn more into the wind and soon the whole sail will be flapping rather than working to create lift.

Remember, a sailboat is similar, yet very different than other boats. You will need to firmly understand the various weaknesses and strengths a sail brings to the table, and act accordingly. Not only for your enjoyment, but for the safety of you, and those you bring with you. Remember the old saying, "The Sea is a Cruel Mistress"

Chapter 3:

Choosing The Right Boat

So, you have a grasp of sailing lingo, maybe you have even attended a sailing school and have time and experience on the open seas. Either way, when you reach the point where you decide you want to obtain a sailboat, there are definitely some factors you will want to consider.

Choosing the right sailboat is definitely an investment. Sailboats are usually distinguished from one another by size, hull configuration, keel type, number and deployment of sails, plus the boat's purpose and use. After considering the functional size needed for your sailboat, you will need to match those features to your sailing tastes. You will also want to select a vessel that you can successfully operate.

The truth is a sailboat is actually a powerboat. In addition to the fine science of a sailboat's design for crisply cutting through waters at a great speed, you will usually find a backup engine for when there is no wind. You will also want to consider the speed of your sailboat. Because your skills will grow quickly once you start sailing frequently, don't buy a boat so safe and stodgy it'll put your grandmother to sleep.

Instead, take some time to find out what boats are popular in your home waters, especially among racing sailors. Even if you have no intentions to race, you'll soon want the performance of a racing sailboat. One thing all sailors enjoy is coaxing more speed from their boats. Doing so is only fun if the speed potential is there to begin with. The better your sailboat performs, the more fun you will have and the more effectively your sailing skills will grow.

Traditional wisdom among sailing experts is to recommend newbies start with a small sailboat. A dinghy or simple sloop is often recommended. A dinghy or simple sloop are single-mast boat with two sails. Because of their size dinghy are recommended so that people can gain the necessary skills to successfully sail and then move up to larger sailboats. Dinghy are easier to maneuver due to fewer lines and number of sails. Smaller sailboats that can easily capsize will teach you to sail very quickly.

Though it sounds counterproductive, knowing how to handle a capsized boat is important. A smaller boat allows one the luxury of knowing how to handle a capsized boat in a controlled environment. Knowing how to handle a capsized boat increases your skillset and is a valuable basic sailing skill. For this reason, it is recommended everyone have experience with a smaller size boat.

However, there is another school of thought on the subject of entering into the world of sailing. Others recommend investing in a small keelboat. A small keelboat is a sailboat in the 22- to 27-foot range. Though this will mean the additional challenge of handling larger sails or more sails, sailboats of this size have many benefits. They are easy to sail, roomy, safe, affordable, and less likely to capsize. Plus, a sailboat in the 22 to 27 foot range will have more room for guests. You will easily be able to carry gear for day-long cruises or even overnight. Usually is a sailboat of this size you will find additional comforts; a head (toilet), refrigerator or ice chest, and maybe even a simple kitchen area.

In addition to the size and features of your sailboat, you will also want to consider the costs. Most people don't realize how affordable boating is: in some instances, you can buy a brand new boat for around **$250.00 a month**. When considering the cost of purchasing a boat you will also want to consider the expenses of several additional factors to help determine your overall budget.

You should estimate the amount of fuel you will use in a year and include this projected expense. You will need to consider the costs of insurance on your sailboat. Keep in mind, often you can reduce the cost of marine insurance premiums by taking a boater's education course.

When determining a sailboat you should also factor in the costs of maintenance. Costs for routine maintenance vary by region, but for more involved services, such as oil changes and winterizing, expect to pay what you would for your car on an hourly basis. You should also remember that due to their age, some pre-owned boats can require significantly more maintenance. In addition, you will want to plan for boat storage. Is a smaller boat you can store in your yard the right match? Or, if you are willing and able to add on the additional expenses that come with storing a boat in a marina or slip then a larger sailboat might be an easier match.

Boats provide tax deductible and cost effective second homes. An interesting point to keep in mind is that sometimes interest on a boat loan can be deducted if the boat has a sleep quarters, a bathroom, and a permanent location at a wharf or dock.

When choosing the right boat, consider the size of the ship you can handle. You also want to keep in mind several other factors to ensure you choose a sailboat that both fits your budget and needs. This will assist in making your purchase a great choice that contributes to your fun and enjoyment in the world of sailing.

Overall, pick a boat you will be happy with and proud to sail and call your own. The connection between a sailor and his ship is a strong one. Your boat will be your escape, your passion and your baby! Take well care of it, and it will take well care of you.

Chapter 4:

Researching Weather Conditions

When sailing a ship on the open seas there are a lot of factors you will need to consider when preparing for your first sailing adventure. Setting out to sea on any type of boat is a big endeavor. However, this should not prevent anyone from learning the sport of sailing and planning their first sailing adventure. Instead, it is important for individuals to be aware of and plan for the many possible scenarios that will come their way.

One factor that can easily be prepared for that will significantly impact a sailing adventure is the weather. Weather conditions will impact a ship's course, the resources sailors will need to bring with them on a voyage, and the strategies needed for a successful sailing adventure. Obviously, different size boats will respond differently to the weather and the ocean. Today's ships have lots of tools that can instantly tell you what the weather conditions are. However, there are a lot of other resources that will aid you in researching weather conditions. Websites, publications and television meteorological reports are all good public resources that can be vital when researching weather conditions for a successful sailing voyage. Here are a few of the weather conditions you might want to consider when preparing for a sailing adventure, plotting your sailboat's course, and choosing your sailing adventure's details.

First, you will want to note the overall temperature. Knowing the temperature of where the ship is sailing will aid you in knowing what type of conditions you might encounter. It is also very important to know precipitation or speed of rainfall in the area where the ship is sailing. With intense rainfall can come increased safety risks.

A key component for any sailboat adventure is obviously wind conditions. Wind speed and direction in the area where the ship is sailing are necessary in planning sailing routes, times, and strategic tactics. The cloud conditions are important for any sailing adventure. You will want to find out if the weather is cloudy or not at the area where the ship is sailing in order to understand what visibility will be. Visibility is important for both the safety of the crew and vessel. With lower visibility additional precautions will be necessary to ensure safety and a successful voyage.

Beyond some basic weather conditions, there are some additional oceanic conditions that you will want to consider when you are on water versus on land. One of these conditions is Wave Height. The wave height in the area where the ship is sailing will definitely impact the ease of maneuverability and effort needed for a sailboat. Smaller boats will feel the impacts of wave height at a greater level than a larger sailboat. The temperature of the sea water in the area where the ship is sailing should also be noted. Not only does the temperature impact as far as weather conditions such as ice, it will also impact other conditions and the responsiveness of the ocean overall. Swell period is the frequency of the swell that happens every time with the second unit at the area where the ship is sailing. You may also find it beneficial to note the swell direction that happens at the area where the ship is sailing as well as swell height. Like wave conditions swell period, directions, and height will largely impact how a sailboat is going to respond to open waters.

Weather will impact all aspects of your voyage. All of these factors are commonly reviewed when planning for a successful sailing adventure. The information from researching a few meteorological conditions can make all the difference between the success or failure of your ship and crew.

Chapter 5:

Learning The Art Of Sail Control

Learning the art of sail control can be a scary thought. After all, the sails are the primary driving force for a sailboat. There is a lot that can be done to control the angle and action on sails. Remembering all of this information can be close to impossible. Instead of trying to learn everything at once, learn a few basic techniques to aid you as you plan your first sailing adventure.

Loosen the shrouds and backstay in order to sail with a loose headstay in light to moderate air. In other words, loosen the sails. This is accomplished by to power up the jib and "decrease" the sheeting angle. On the contrary, Sail with a tight sail in breeze to de-power or flatten the jib and "increase" the sheeting angle. Do this by tightening the shrouds. The shroud is the set of ropes supporting the mast. By tightening these ropes the sails angle becomes tightened or increased.

If wind is low, slant the mast forward to increase the chord length on the sails and close up the slot between the jib and main. This will allow the sails to maximize the wind that is available. However, if winds are stronger the mast should rake, or slant backwards or aft. This will shorn the rope length on the sails and open up the slot between the jib and main.

If winds are light, induce mast bend with the standing rigging to flatten the front of the main. You will want to give slack to allow sails to perform at their fullest. Of course, the opposite will hold true if winds are stronger. You will want to prevent mast bend with the standing rigging as sail tension will bend the mast enough. The movement of the mast impacts the power of the sailboat. In ideal conditions, mast bend is not necessary because a straight mast creates a powerful sail. However, weather and wind conditions fluctuate requiring us to move the sails and mast in order to maximize wind capturing capacity.

When sailing upwind, adjust trim the middle of the jib leech parallel with the centerline of the boat in moderate air. The jib leech is the free corner of a sail that is farthest from the mast. If winds are light and/or heavy you will want to twist the leech or claw as it is also known.

When sailing upwind, adjust the top batten of the main so that it id parallel with the boom. This will enable you to maximize sail potential. However, in moderate air, twist the leach open in light or heavy air to allow both security and increased potential in the sails.

When working on a sailboat, much of the adjustments will involve using ropes to do so. An important component to sailing is knowing how to secure lines. This is accomplished by a variety of knots.

A reef knot or square knot is used to shorten sails when winds are too strong. The square knot is made by twisting 2 ends of line together as if you've started to tie your shoe, right over left. Next go left over right. It's done right if both bitter ends come out of the knot on the same side. This knot can also be used to tie together 2 different lines of the same diameter. It is a quite common and useful nautical knot.

If you are working with ropes of different diameters you will need to use a sheet bend knot in order to tie the 2 lines together. First you will need to form a loop in the large line, the loop coming over the top. Push the bitter end, or end of line, for the smaller line up from below the loop, around the standing end of the larger line, then back in the hole. Draw tightly.

You will also want to know how to tie your sailboat to a dock. This is done by using a bow line. You will wrap the rope around a stanchion either once or twice. Next, loop the loose end once over the standing part. Loop again and thread the loose end between the 2 coils on the standing end and pull tightly.

It is important to keep in mind that every time you put a knot in a line you weaken it, so putting extra twists and bends in the line to make a knot more secure is actually counterproductive. Instead, using the right knot for the right situation gives the strength needed in the appropriate situation.

Chapter 6:

Additional Tips

Planning your first sailing adventure is an exciting endeavor. Preparation will make the adventure a smooth one. As a beginner, there are some additional tips you should keep in mind.

Choose calm, uncrowded waters if you're just starting out with master sailing basics and learn how to sail, this important as a beginner. You will want to practice in ideal conditions so you can focus on learning to sail. Research weather conditions before you leave to ensure you have adequate provisions.

Never sail alone, especially when you are first starting out and learning the ropes, literally. Having another person on board ensures an extra set of hands for unexpected situations and emergencies. It is strongly recommended to bring a more experienced sailor with you until you have a firm and fluent understanding of all that can happen to you and your boat.

Never stop learning. Don't be afraid to ask more experienced sailors for advice. Better yet, ask such sailors if you could go for a sail with them sometime. Almost all sailors will be more than happy to teach you some things they have learned over the years. Each person brings something new to teach, as each person has had different experiences at sea, good or bad.

Remain calm and follow sailing basics for safety purposes. There are several logical sailing basics for safe boating that should follow no matter what your level of expertise. For example, always telling someone before you go out on the water, always bringing a floatation device, bring emergency preparation items such as flares, a first aid kit, and food items. Also, know how to swim.

A few basic sailing skills will go a long way. One, become familiar with sail control. Successful sailors are the ones who are able to adjust sail settings to take the advantage of different wind and water conditions. In general, sails should be relatively flat when the wind is either very light or very strong, and full when there is a moderate wind. Also, always remember...respect the boom. Always be aware of its presence and direction. Some of the most common sailing injuries are a result of not being aware when the boom is about to swing.

Sailing can be a great past time, just remember, practice makes perfect. Don't try to teach yourself all the sailing basics. No one can learn everything alone. Instead, attend a good sailing course and do your research. Read guides and books, and learn from experienced sailors.

Conclusion

Thank you again for downloading this book!

I hope this book was able to help you to plan your first sailing adventure.

The next step is to get out there and start learning how to sail.

Finally, if you enjoyed this book, then I'd like to ask you for a favor, would you be kind enough to leave a review for this book on Amazon? I am always looking for feedback and recommendations for future books! It'd be greatly appreciated!

Click here to leave a review for this book on Amazon!

Thank you and good luck!

Printed in Great Britain
by Amazon